From East to West
Growing up in East Germany

Karin Ashby

FROM EAST TO WEST

Copyright © 2020 Karin Ashby
All rights reserved.
ISBN: 9798654236111

DEDICATION

For my husband Keith and all our family: four children - Kristin, Mark, Nicky and Katrin - nine grandchildren and now great-grandchildren. With great gratitude and in the hope that they might be interested to learn a little more about their German roots.

FROM EAST TO WEST

FOREWORD

84 years ago on 5th March 1936 Karin Engelhardt was born. 84 years ago in 1936 Joseph Stalin came to power in Russia. 84 years ago in 1936 Butlin's first holiday camp opened in Skegness.

67 years ago on 5th March 1953 Stalin died and Karin celebrated in East Germany and so became an Enemy of the State. Whereupon she decided to get out of East Germany and become an Air Hostess for Lufthansa in the West.

It takes some enterprise and courage to go abroad aged 18, NOT knowing the foreign country, NOT knowing anyone there, NOT knowing the language. That is the sort of person she is.

The following is a record of her memories and thoughts from that far away period.

Keith Ashby
April 2020

FROM EAST TO WEST

Mönchen-
gladbach

Eisenach

Berlin

Hagen

EAST GERMANY

WEST GERMANY

FROM EAST TO WEST

From East to West
Growing up in East Germany

The Russians burst into our house, shouting "Razzia". They were checking for guns and ammunition but my grandmother thought they were after her sausages. "Quick! Hide them!" She gave me a stick laden with rings of Knackwurst, years old, to hide. So I put them in my bed! My grandmother owned a small butcher's shop and these sausages had been hidden away, only to be eaten in an emergency.

I can't remember when I came to live with my grandmother but it might have been in 1942, when I was six. My parents lived in Hagen, where my father was proud owner of a printing press. But Hagen was situated at the heart of German industry and bombs began falling dangerously close to our flat. So one day I heard my mother say, "It's time for her to go to Eisenach. It just isn't safe here anymore." So I said good-bye to my friends and to a special boy I had always played with. I still have scars on my knees to show the tough games we used to play in the streets and in bombed-out houses. But going on a journey was more exciting than that, or so I thought at the time.

My sister, Inge, was six years older than me and I hardly

remember her being in Hagen, for she was often away on youth camps with the Bund Deutscher Mädchen (League of German Girls), which was the equivalent for girls of the Hitler Youth. These camps took place in Czechoslovakia, so the family were split up.

Inge and Karin

My grandmother, Karolina or Lina, as she was called, was a formidable woman with little sense of humour, so hardly a suitable person to look after a six year old. But this was wartime and physical safety counted for more than anything.

Karolina aka Lina

We lived in Goldschmiedenstrasse 32 (32 Goldsmith Street) and when my grandfather, Paul, was still alive there was a Jewish family living opposite. Apparently they were a nice quiet family, but my grandmother heard from a friend that Jewish businesses were being destroyed and their occupants arrested, so my grandparents decided to hide these neighbours. On Kristallnacht in 1938 their jewellery shop was smashed up and their house searched, but they were hidden in my grandparents' house and were not caught.

Paul (grandfather)

My grandmother lived in a large old house from which she ran a butcher's shop. It had stables, haylofts and a washhouse leading off a small courtyard. A few rooms at the top of the house were let to an elderly lady, Fräulein Lange. But there were still many empty rooms, so my grandmother thought she would take in a couple as lodgers. After a few months she noticed that the lock of a special trunk in which she kept sheets, tablecloths and other linen had been tampered with. When she found that most of her best linen had been stolen, the police were called. They could not find the thief and were getting quite threatening until the thief's wife told them where to look. One particular room had a long wall cupboard, very low and not easy to see. He was hiding in that and had crawled to the very end of it, so they had to get him out by poking him with a broom handle. This was all very exciting, I thought.

So was the incident of the man who decided to hide behind a heavy curtain near the shop door. When shutting up shop for the night my grandmother found him hiding there. I saw him running past the shop as for his life. No doubt he hadn't allowed for my grandmother's temper. She had probably given him a few punches to see him on his way. She was not going to let herself be robbed again.

I used to help my grandmother to collect meat and sausages from a larger shop which supplied her with the goods to sell in her own shop. One day I went to the station with a rickety handcart to collect a deer to be sold in the shop. The eyes of the deer stared at me vacantly and I hurried home, afraid lest the beast might suddenly spring to life.

In the shop a special trick of my grandmother's was to add a few cupfuls of water to the minced meat, so that it weighed more, which made it more profitable to sell. Sometimes she got a bit carried away with the watering and had to add salt to bind the meat together. The customers seemed happy though, not noticing or pretending not to notice. Food was becoming quite scarce and when the meat had gone there was nothing else to sell in the shop except a kind of gravy mixture.

My grandmother also taught me how to fiddle the scales by twiddling a knob at the side which made the goods appear heavier than they were. When the inspector came unannounced she would pacify him with a piece of sausage kept back for just such occasions.

Goldschmiedenstrasse 32

What I hated most in the shop was sticking stamps from the ration books into booklets. Tiny bits of paper were blown about when I sneezed or when someone opened a door. And there was a very pungent smell from the glue.

Every day at a certain time the electricity was switched off and we had to use paraffin lamps, which sounds romantic but is rather smelly and dirty. The shade had to be cleaned daily, as the paraffin left a black sooty grease stain and this left the shop very dingy on winter evenings.

I started school in Eisenach and made many new friends. Together we would go out to explore the countryside round Eisenach.

Wartburg Castle, Eisenach

I also went for long walks with my grandmother when we would take with us a picnic of bread and sausage. In winter we would take the cart to collect wood, which was becoming scarce, and in the summer we would collect quantities of blueberries, which we ate cold with milk and sugar or hot with yeast dumplings.

I started to add up bills in the back room, but that was soon to stop, as my grandmother was convinced that I could become almost perfect in rattling off the times tables. There was no mercy for me. Tucked up in bed at 9 o'clock I could not remember my 8 times table, so I had to get out of my nice warm bed and recite it over and over again until I could remember it. And I still do remember my times tables, though only in German.

Paul, Inge, Lina, Ilse (aunt) and Frida (mother)

When Polish prisoners of war arrived in Germany, tired and hungry, my grandmother decided to take them under her wing. So I had to collect old potatoes from various friends, again using the handcart, pulling and tugging it up and down the hills around Eisenach. She used these potatoes to make a delicious potato salad for them. I still use the same recipe now, though with added mayonnaise.

Recipe: Boil potatoes in their skins, leave to cool, peel, add a cornflour sauce mixed with mayonnaise, pour over potatoes, add a chopped onion, season with pepper and salt, decorate with tomatoes, hard-boiled eggs, parsley, etc.

The prisoners were forbidden to buy goods of any sort in the local shops, so she made them queue quietly at the back of the shop. They then handed her one Reichsmark and the packets of potato salad, which were all ready for them under the counter, were handed out. When she felt very generous, she would slip the odd piece of sausage into the parcels. It was just as well that nobody reported her, because quite likely it would have been the concentration camp for both of us. Years after the war I visited Buchenwald, which was very near Eisenach and thought of my grandmother and those Polish prisoners. But in 1945, when the war was over, and she wanted to give some sausage to the prisoners they just laughed at her and gave it back.

Once a week my grandmother scooped me up to take me to the cemetery to put flowers on the grave of my grandfather. We left in a wobbly old tram which shook and coughed alarmingly. We collected water for the plants on the grave from a communal fountain and pulled out any weeds. My grandmother talked to my grandfather and made me greet him on arrival. I was fascinated by the various gravestones, which ranged from one month old infants surrounded by angels to family graves behind iron railings hundreds of years old. Then we walked round the graveyard and my grandmother pointed out the graves of her friends and relatives. Some were neglected, so I had to pull out the weeds from those as well. Everybody kept their vases and watering cans behind their gravestones ready for use. Once we had said good-bye to my grandfather we clanked back in the tram, worn out and ready for our supper.

I found it strange that she was suddenly so fond of my grandfather, as I had heard people saying that in his lifetime he was more interested in joining his friends in shooting parties and that, on coming home from the shoot, he would spend all night in the pub, sleeping in next morning and leaving my grandmother to cope with the shop. This was a big job, for at that time they employed several butcher apprentices and maids, killing their own meat, making sausages and smoking meats. But it seems all was forgiven when he died.

Paul, founder of the hunting association on its 25th anniversary

My grandmother loved music and often went to the theatre with her friends to see plays or listen to her beloved Strauss and Lehar waltzes. On one occasion my grandfather had got some friends to help him push the pub piano down the road and played Happy Birthday to her outside in the street. But my grandmother was not amused, as it was 3 o'clock in the morning and his friends in the street were quite drunk.

To my delight, in 1944 my mother and sister came to join us in Eisenach. The camps and hostels where my sister had been staying were becoming increasingly unsafe as the war progressed. This meant my father was now living alone with his printing press in Hagen, surrounded by bombed-out buildings.

Inge, Frida, Karin and Ilse

With the arrival of my mother came a new bathroom, as my mother was not prepared to live in a house without one. It was installed next to my grandmother's room, an enormous cast-iron bathtub and a huge cylindrical stove which had to be fed with coal and wood to heat the water. This was quite a complicated performance, which meant that bath time came only once a week. On Saturday, after shutting up shop, came the ritual of lighting the stove. We all made the most of that bath and emerged hot, pink and clean. To save fuel we shared the water, so it was first come, first served, but mother always came last – good old mum.

Karin and Inge

A friend from Hagen, Frau Krone, wrote to say that she and her daughter Gisela would like to stay with us in Eisenach, as the air raids in Hagen were becoming horrendous. Frau Krone's husband was away fighting in the war and so they were alone in Hagen with the bombing. Frau Krone was rather a neurotic type - perhaps the war had made her so - and as soon as the siren went off she would insist on taking Gisela and my sister and me to a nearby brewery, which was built into a hill and served as an air raid shelter. I used to carry my brown leather case, containing my best dress, a few odds and ends and my gas mask. People all congregated in that cellar, laughing and singing Hitler songs, sharing their food and playing cards. The radio loudspeaker was still blaring out Hitler's speeches of how he was winning the war when the Americans marched into Eisenach.

We emerged rather dazed and numb to find the war was over. It was a beautiful day as we walked back to our house, where my mother and grandmother had stayed, "preferring to die in comfort" as my mother said. All along the road people had taken in their German Nazi flags and hung out of the windows the white sheets of surrender. "Feeble lot," I thought.

The Americans seemed quite harmless, not the ogres they were portrayed as in Hitler's propaganda. They distributed sweets and chocolate among the children - goodies which no one had tasted for years. Children flocked round them and looked very happy as they chewed away, but I was told that under no circumstances was I to go anywhere near the soldiers, so I stood on the opposite pavement watching the sweets being handed out and not feeling very happy at all.

I went to do some shopping with my mother, hoping some

sweets might have reached the shops, when to the horror of myself and the shopkeeper, I heard my mother address everyone with a "Heil Hitler". Old habits die hard!

One evening there came a knock at the door. My father was standing in the street, having cycled all the way from Hagen on a stolen bike, being shot at on the way, avoiding arrest and starving. He looked terrible, having lost a lot of weight on the way. We were all thrilled to see him and a feast was prepared, which I remember to this day: a schnitzel each, cauliflower in a sauce which was as near as we could get to white sauce when there was no white flour, followed by a flan filled with slightly fermenting fruit, topped with ersatz cream, made of beaten egg white. It all tasted delicious, but my father had a sad tale to tell. His beloved printing press had been destroyed in the bombing and all his machinery and life savings were lost.

Hermann (father)

Then Frau Krone's husband arrived back safely from the war. He told us incredible tales of his experiences and brought back some disgusting-tasting sweets from Denmark. How disappointed we were after seeing the delicious sweets the American soldiers were handing out. But we all lived together quite happily, having enough food for all of us, thanks to the little butcher's shop.

But then a terrible rumour became reality. The American troops had suddenly left by night and Eisenach was to be taken over by the Russians. Horrified people scuttled about, locking doors and hiding themselves away. There was no hiding for us though, as we had to keep the shop open. My father needed some cigars to steady his nerves, so I had to fetch some from the shop next door. As I waited to be served, a Russian officer came into the shop, sending everyone into a panic. Nothing happened though and the Russian officer left with his cigars, looking most embarrassed.

After that an endless stream of Russian soldiers marched and rode past, while people were watching from their windows. I suddenly remembered Hitler's saying that all enemies had to be wiped out, so I decided to spit the disgusting Danish sweets on to the soldiers. Luckily for me neither the soldiers nor my parents noticed.

It was then that the Russian soldiers burst into all the houses shouting "Razzia" and searching for weapons and ammunition. "Open the doors," they demanded, so we did, though my mother and sister quickly went into hiding and my grandmother disappeared to collect the sausages which she gave to me to hide. She had saved these sausages for ages and was not giving them away to anybody. But, for goodness sake, where was I to hide them? I ran upstairs and put them in my bed and then went to hide in one of the rooms rented by Fräulein Lange. As the soldiers rushed upstairs they came to Fräulein Lange's room and seeing the terrified old lady presumed she rented all the rooms. They didn't think she had anything to hide and left, nearly falling down the narrow staircase. Phew! What a relief. The sausages were safe. I was reminded of that incident for weeks, as the smoky smell lingered on in my bed, for sheets and duvet covers were washed only once a month.

The food shortages were becoming increasingly severe. Even bread and butter were becoming scarce but could be exchanged for meat. Once I bought some meat on the black market to be resold in the shop, but as I came near my mother waved me on, as there were police in the shop, looking for just such black market dealings. I walked several times round the block until it was safe to enter the shop with my ill-gotten purchases.

As food was scarce my mother's friends sometimes came round for a meal, for we were protected from the worst of the shortages because of the shop. On one occasion the husband did not seem to mind the maggots floating about in his porridge and quietly arranged them on the edge of his plate while I looked on in horror. The oats were probably several years old but still considered edible, more or less.

Frida (second from left) and friends

We were all busy in the shop one Saturday morning when a woman customer told my mother how ill she felt. "Come along then," my mother said. "You can have a rest in my bed until you feel better." My sister and I were amazed. We certainly wouldn't have let a stranger sleep in our beds. But when the woman, who was a farmer's wife, came back a day or two later with some whipping cream in thanks we were delighted with our mother for being so kind.

Our house was surrounded, on both sides and opposite, by shops, so when anything worth buying was being unloaded we were first at hand to catch some of those goods. Lavatory paper especially was in short supply, so I was sent from shop to shop to buy as many rolls as possible. There were no bananas, of course, or citrus fruit, except occasionally an odd lemon. Then I would run as quickly as I could to buy one, for only one was allowed per family, no more. We could buy local worm-eaten apples, lettuces with greenfly and Bulgarian gherkins in jars. Sometimes there was even the odd cauliflower. Often goods were being kept for us under the counter and I had strict instructions to bring home whatever was offered. It was always worthwhile to keep on the friendly side of us and our sausages!

Unfortunately one friendship was broken forever. A few Russian soldiers were out on the prowl looking for girls. As they were knocking on everyone's door, all locked and bolted, we heard our neighbour tell the soldiers they had no girls in their house, but there were some next door, pointing to our house. As my sister and I were hustled into the cellar by our mother, our grandmother glared at the soldiers from an upstairs window, ready to pour boiling oil over them. That was enough to make them leave hastily to try another door. A nasty incident, though, which left us rather frightened. No one from our house ever spoke to those neighbours again. It was their loss though, for they sold flowers and what were they compared to our sausages!

While all goods were in short supply, building materials were virtually non-existent, so when a leak occurred in our roof we did not know what to do. It was a flat roof, which was covered by sheets of tarred paper and with wooden slats on top. Suddenly my grandmother had an idea. She had seen a pile of tar pieces outside the Russian Embassy next to the theatre. We had to get that tar to be melted down for our roof. So one dark night she took the cart and me and we set off to steal from the pile. My parents were at home nearly having a fit, but I had no choice, so off we went. We loaded the cart with the tar pieces. It was a freezing night but both my grandmother and I were feeling quite hot, waiting for someone to discover our evil plan. However all went well, my father melted the tar down and our roof stopped leaking.

Eisenach Theatre (to its left is the Russian Embassy where Karin and her grandmother stole tar to mend their roof)

A curfew was enforced, forbidding everyone from going out in the evenings. So I was stuck in the house every evening, and not able to meet my friends. I used to run out of the house to the street corner and back, just to break the curfew. But it was quite creepy going out into a completely deserted street, for not even animals were allowed out.

A stream of German refugees from Czechoslovakia began to be seen, forlornly dragging their few belongings down the streets of Eisenach. They were mostly just women and children, their husbands and fathers having been lost in the war. They were relying on strangers to open their doors to them and take them in. Such a family, a couple and their grown up daughter knocked on our door one day. "Can we stay with you?" the husband asked, looking most embarrassed. "Of course you can," my mother assured them, so they lived with us for several months. They had been mill owners and had left all their wealth behind and now relied on our charity. It must have been quite dreadful for them. In the end they left for West Germany to stay with relatives.

My father had by now set up his own workshop, where he employed four or five women to make boxes for cakes and soles for shoes. As he had been a member of the Nazi party he was not given permission to start another printing press which he would have loved to have done. His workshop was in one of the outhouses which were used to store the equipment for the once flourishing butcher's shop. The women were happy working for him as he had a good sense of humour. He managed to get hold of a few books on palmistry and women came flocking to have their palms read. He was quite enjoying all the attention, especially as my mother did not think too much of "all that hocus pocus" as she called it. One day a woman brought him a pound of butter, as his predictions had come true and she was very pleased. We never did find out what he had told her.

Meanwhile, the day to day chores had to be seen to. There was the monthly wash, which took place with much protest from my mother, in the washhouse downstairs. The fire was lit at 6 a.m. under a huge copper cauldron and in that everything was boiled from underclothes to bed linen. What a performance. Huge sheets were taken from the bubbling mass to be put into a hand-operated washing machine, whose lever had to be pushed back and forth fifty times during the process. Then it all went through a mangle to press out the water, then back into another huge container to be rinsed. Then back through the mangle, then carried all through the house to be hung either on the open roof or inside the covered roof space when it rained. Then down again to collect the second lot, back up three flights of stairs, the last so narrow and winding it would have been quite easy to lose one's step and fall down, especially as Fräulein Lange, our lodger, kept these stairs polished to perfection.

Next to the washhouse was the freezer room, containing enormous fridges where meat was kept cold by huge blocks of ice. This room was very well insulated and kept the cold air out in the winter so that my grandmother thought we should keep chickens in there. They were allowed out to scratch around in the yard, which was concreted, so they mostly scratched around in the boxes in which my father grew tobacco leaves. It was my job to collect grass and greens for them to eat, so they became pets and I liked to stroke them. But the day came when, having failed to lay the required number of eggs, my grandmother had the hens killed. When they were cooked and appeared on the Sunday lunch table, everyone suddenly seemed to have lost their appetite.

Meanwhile the black market flourished. There was very little alcohol to be had, so my uncle, who was a well-known dentist in the town, decided to make schnapps in the washhouse. Once again I was sent out with the wobbly handcart to collect old potatoes from friends and neighbours. The fomenting potatoes gave off the most pungent smell, so we had to keep the front door locked at all times. The police must not get wind of the illegal schnapps making. My uncle's plan was to sell the schnapps to the Russians living in his house, for the Russian officers and their families were now living in the pretty houses in Eisenach's suburbia, leaving us in our rambling old townhouse alone, thank goodness.

There was great excitement when the long-closed cinemas were opened up again. So my friends and I went to see many old classics, including some very good Russian films. It was our only form of entertainment. But there was a big snag. We none of us had any money. Our pocket money didn't stretch that far. Suddenly I had the bright idea of selling my sister's books. I didn't own any books, so it had to be hers. All her beloved 'Pücksibücher' went to a second-hand bookshop whose owner was very pleased indeed, giving us a very modest payment for the books. My sister was heartbroken, there was a great row and my mother tried in vain to buy the books back.

Karin and Inge

My uncle and his family had by now moved back into their own house, for the Russian officer who had been occupying it had moved out. My uncle had long grown tired of living in East Germany and had arranged for his wife and two children and his dentist's chair to be smuggled into West Germany on a farm truck. They had already left, with my aunt disguised as a farmer's wife. He was about to leave himself when he woke up terrified to find a Russian standing by his bed. Thinking he had come to take him away, as had happened to so many people, he was more than a little relieved to hear that the Russian had toothache and wanted my uncle to look at his teeth. He had let himself in, having kept a key to the house which he had previously occupied.

My uncle left next morning, leaving all the furniture, pictures, carpets and his car behind. My grandmother was heartbroken, seeing the things she had saved for to ensure a bottom drawer for my aunt being left to whoever wanted them. Our family were not allowed to touch anything in the house, as my father wanted to leave the eastern sector as well, but my mother preferred to stay where we were in the old house with the butcher's shop and so we did not go.

My friends and I had a lot of spare time, as school finished at 1 o'clock and sometimes we got into trouble. There was an open air concert hall in Eisenach, the Karthaus Garten, to which my grandmother would go happily with her friends to hear her favourite music. The concert hall was set in a beautiful park and people walked around and admired the flowers while listening to the music. The concerts were always well attended, especially on warm summer nights, and my friends and I got a good telling off one evening from the park attendant when he caught us climbing over a fence to avoid paying.

)ther time I remember dazzling a neighbour with a mirror while she was making dumplings. She became so exasperated that she threw a dumpling at me which hit the window. Another time I was playing at hairdressers with a friend and for some reason threw a mirror out of the window which landed in the street, narrowly missing a policeman. He promptly came upstairs looking for us. We managed to rush up to the flat roof of the house and hid behind a chimney. We were not found, thank goodness, and Fräulein Lange did not give us away.

I spent a good deal of time with Fräulein Lange listening to her stories of her childhood. She had, hanging from a lamp, a rather nice Steiff teddy bear, which she promised to leave to me when she died. I checked up daily to see if she had died so I could have the bear! When she did die years later I had left Eisenach, so I expect the teddy bear got thrown away.

She used to scrape the food out of her saucepans with amazing gusto, so as not to waste a scrap, and the noise could be heard all through the house. My father called this strange scratching noise "The Fräulein Lange Waltz".

Time was slipping by and I was nearly ready for my Confirmation. More important to me than the religious ceremony was the feast to come. A cook was hired, piles of cakes were baked, glasses washed and silver polished. Several women came to clean the house and polish the furniture, while curtains were washed and sent to be ironed. Friends and relatives arrived and we all went to church dressed in black. Our stamp books were collected, for each of us who had attended church was given a weekly stamp.

Then the questioning started. The congregation were amazed at our knowledge of the Bible, for questions were flung at us and answered in seconds, all hands going up. What the congregation didn't know was that if we didn't know the answer to a question we were told to put up our hand anyway but with a finger crooked. Then we would not be asked. When the ceremony was over we rushed home to have lunch. Then it was time to take a plate of cakes to neighbours in the street. Flowers kept arriving through the afternoon and it was all very exciting.

Georgenkirche (St George's Church), Eisenach, where J. S. Bach was baptised

But the highlight for me was that I could now have my long plaits cut off. So the day after the Confirmation my friends and I rushed to have our hair cut short. We had to keep our plaits for the Confirmation ceremony, for that was the tradition. However, after having my hair cut I felt it would have been more sensible to have listened to my mother and kept the plaits as they were. I looked horrendous, my hair standing up in a frizzy mess. I sneaked home dejectedly and went to bed. But it looked just as frightful when I woke up next morning.

Sports gear was beginning to appear in the shops, for the state was keen to encourage any kind of sport. There were ski huts and hotels for the use of the young, and especially of the Young Pioneers and the older section, the Free German Youth. I flatly refused to join either group and so did my friends and we looked down on the girls who joined. Fortunately for us in the early stages everyone could use the facilities. I was fortunate to know the owner of a shop where I bought a nice pair of skis and joined the ski club. A few friends joined as well and on Sunday morning at 4.48 we all left to go to Oberhof.

Skiing at Oberhof

Resting after skiing on skis – no ski lifts!

There were no lessons for us or ski lifts, so we just struggled on as best we could. But we had a good time, eating our snow-covered sandwiches and drinking water from a nearby stream. On the way back we sat in our wet clothes in an unheated train and sang to keep ourselves warm. Quite a tough lot we were, I should say. I was also lucky to find a pair of ice skates in a tree and could not resist taking them. They were rather old but what did that matter? I managed to tie them to my shoes, my boots having been stolen by someone wandering around in our house. My best boots those were too.

Christmas was approaching and there was very little in the shops, so a friend and I decided to go to the western sector to do our Christmas shopping. It was comparatively easy to leave the eastern sector then. We just had to apply for a passport which was handed back on return. Schnapps was not scarce anymore, so we decided to obtain our passports, buy some schnapps, sell it in the west and with that money buy our Christmas presents – all highly illegal, but quite exciting. We cycled to Kassel, a town in the west, and were lucky to sell most of our bottles, so we were able to buy all sorts of small presents. Very pleased with ourselves, we arrived home rather late. My mother meanwhile was frantic with worry. As I put my bag down to open the door, my last bottle of schnapps broke, pouring schnapps everywhere.

I was myself becoming more and more discontented with living in East Germany, as friends were leaving and my sister and her boyfriend were thinking of leaving too. Then an incident occurred which could have stopped me from leaving altogether. I had been to stay with my uncle and aunt and was full of praise for the West, where there was so much in the shops, while in the East there were shortages of everything, queues for everything. So when one day our Russian teacher told us how underprivileged people were in West Germany I, like a fool, spoke up, saying I thought otherwise. The Russian teacher and a Communist Party member turned up that evening at my grandmother's shop and told my mother that I was not to go back to school, that I was suspended. My father, who until this incident, had avoided becoming a member of the Communist Party, quickly joined and protested to the authorities, telling them that I was still young and hardly responsible for my action. So after four weeks of non-school I was allowed back. But I flatly refused to join the Young Pioneers, a political organisation peppering children with Communist propaganda.

Class at School (Karin is fourth from left in second row from the top)

I took private lessons in English and French, decided that I would like to go to those countries and eventually become an air hostess.

Meanwhile it was time to change school. The local Gymnasium (high school) in Eisenach was out of bounds for me and some of my property-owning non-proletariat friends. I was quite proud of being thought a capitalist thanks to my grandmother's tiny butcher's shop. She was hardly a wealthy shop owner! I could have gone to a Gymnasium in Ruhla, an hour's train ride from Eisenach, but my mother was horrified at the thought of my having to travel two hours by train every day. So I ended up going to the technical school in Eisenach learning book-keeping, shorthand and typing. I quite hated being at that school, as all my friends were at other schools, for their parents did not mind them travelling by train. And I was bored by learning the skills necessary for office work.

Eventually I got a job in an office, my first job, taking over from a secretary who had been with my boss for twenty-five years. Poor man, he was quite devastated, especially as I could not always make out my own shorthand and wrote the strangest letters to firms, asking them to collect goods in Eisenach which weren't even there. They would be delighted when they thought they had found some spare parts and come hurrying round only to be told this was not so.

My boss soon realised office work was not for me and found me a place at a college for teachers of physical training. So it was a question of either accepting a place at the college or leaving for West Germany in order to get a passport which would enable me to go to Britain. As I had found a family in West Germany who were willing to take me on as a 'house daughter' for one year I chose to leave. The East German passport and currency were not recognised or accepted in the West, so I had to stay in West Germany one year to obtain a passport that would be acceptable.

A few years later, on returning to Eisenach, I thought I should visit my former boss and was told he had committed suicide. I was very sorry to hear that and also felt slightly guilty, first for having been so hopeless at my job and then for having left for the West, something perhaps he would have liked to do himself.

Everything was being arranged for my journey to Mönchengladbach. My mother insisted that I should wear a hat on my journey. Every nice girl wore a hat on journeys.

How I hated hats. I think she tried as hard as possible to make things difficult for me, so as to make me change my mind and stay in the East. She even promised to buy a car for me, something I had always longed for. It was no easy matter to get hold of a car in the eastern sector, where parents put their children's names down at birth to qualify for buying a car at the age of sixteen or eighteen. I shudder to think how many sausages it would have cost to bribe people into letting us have a car. Money was not the problem but the goods simply weren't available. People were waiting years to own a washing machine and many years later I visited a friend in the East, who proudly showed off the caravan which she and her husband had at last managed to get hold of.

A snazzy two piece suit was made for me. The material was rather heavy and I remember feeling quite tired when wearing it. My mother thought the material contained wood fibre, so I left for West Germany carrying half the Thüringer Wald on my shoulders.

I arrived in Mönchengladbach to live with a dentist's family as their 'house daughter', as they called it. I called it something else after finding out that I was just a glorified maid, who cleaned, washed, got their three school-aged children ready for school, had to get up at 6 o'clock to get their breakfast and supervise their leaving for school – me, who had to be supervised myself or so my mother thought. When it came to cleaning the flat, Frau König was not amused to watch me in what I thought was perfectly adequate cleaning, especially as the flat didn't look dirty anyway. Instead of just a quick flick with a duster, ornaments had to be moved and the last straw was that I had to comb the fringes of the carpets when they became ruffled during hoovering. Having had a cleaning woman at home, I thought back longingly to the days of skiing and playing tennis. But there was no going back to the East. Having left, I was now an enemy of the state, which meant staying put. I might be allowed to visit after a lapse of two years with the consent of the East German government. That meant filling out four forms with all sorts of details, as I found out later.

Meanwhile I had to struggle with my house-daughterly duties. Washday was not quite so bad as at home, as the König family had a few of the latest gadgets, but I had endless dentists' coats to struggle with and ironing was another nightmare. The beastly white coats took ages and there were so many shirts. The handkerchiefs had to be folded in a special way, as did the serviettes. But I soon learned to be a reasonable house daughter. The family was really very tolerant and we even had the odd laugh, especially as it seemed to have become a habit of mine to weep quietly every night over my supper, tears running on to my plate. After a while they got used to my strange habits and we just laughed the whole thing off. Being with that family must have been the closest I ever came to being at a finishing school. The family were Catholic, so on Sundays off went the children to church, but the parents preferred to have a lie in.

My year was quickly over and I hadn't fared too badly, being nearly a qualified Hausfrau. Meanwhile my English teacher had found a family in Cambridge who were looking for a German au pair girl. Everything was arranged, tickets bought, but, alas, there was a train strike in England and I had to wait a little longer. Frau König seemed quite glad to have me staying on and I certainly was, for where could I have gone? My substitute arrived, also from East Germany, a girl just as hopeless at housework as I was, as it turned out. What a chore it must have been to have to train all these young girls from the East.

The rail strike was over and I was ready to leave. Everyone came to see me off at the station, hankies were waved, last good-byes said, so England here I come.

The journey to Cambridge was quite uneventful. I vaguely remember meeting a girl in the train, who was also au pairing. I said good-bye to the girl in London, but she was looking extremely worried, as there seemed to be no one there to collect her.

At last the train arrived in Cambridge. I was met, thank goodness, by my English family, Dr. and Mrs. Keats. They turned out to be extremely friendly people and so were their three boys. And they were very understanding too, as they tried to piece together my strange-sounding English. How I wished I had worked harder on my English lessons in Eisenach, learning my English vocabulary, rather than tobogganing down the hill on which my teacher lived.

Life in Cambridge was a lot of fun. I had very little to do in the house, as a cleaning woman came in to do most of the work. Also the English housewife does not seem as obsessed with housework as the German Hausfrau. Phew, what a relief. No more combing of the carpet fringes. I was feeling very happy indeed, when I might have been feeling like a stranger in a foreign country, speaking a different language and experiencing a different way of living. And it was so soon after the war too. I was nineteen in 1955 and soon began to grow very fond of the English and their language.

Karin at 18

One thing puzzled me. Why were all the children wearing the same clothes? I fetched one of the boys from school one day and felt confused by seeing all the pupils dressed alike. In East Germany we saw people wearing identical dresses, bought off the peg, manufactured by the thousands, and found that very embarrassing indeed. My English teacher must have mentioned the wearing of uniform by schoolchildren but perhaps I was dreaming during that lesson. Another thing that puzzled me was that the eldest boy in the family was a boarder at a public school, which was only about ten minutes away from where he lived, so within easy walking distance. It seemed very strange indeed. But then I remembered a little 'sticker of advice' in my passport, which said 'Accept the different habits of foreign countries or go back to your own.' That was a wise saying and I acted accordingly.

We all played tennis in the garden and watched cricket, and of course we watched television too, something we had not had at home in East Germany. My principal task was to keep the dining table polished and I had an electric polisher to help me with that. The Keats family also owned a rather marvellous Bendix washing machine, so no more washing day sessions. And English food was so much easier to cook than German food. No elaborate sauces to go with everything, just a great joint of meat every day. And all those delicious biscuits with their endless cups of tea. Some meals were not so enjoyable though. I had to get used to frequent joints of lamb. Lamb is hardly ever eaten in Germany and I first swallowed the pieces whole, too embarrassed to complain. I was also given enormous helpings. Mrs. Keats had been told that all Germans eat vast amounts. But that was phased out after a while, as she found that I couldn't possibly eat all that I was given.

There were hundreds of foreign girls in Cambridge of all nationalities. We used to meet and have coffee at the Alexandra House, now pulled down to make way for new shops. What a pity. There was an au pair called Hilda from West Germany living in the same street as me, so we met up and hitch-hiked all over the place. She was staying with a Jewish family with the very German-sounding name of Schlossmann, but as they grew up two of the family, Werner and Peter, changed their name to Shawdon, which sounded much more English, and later Werner preferred to be known by his middle name of Arthur, so that sounded even more English, though he still kept his German accent

Karin, Danish girl and Hilda

Karin and Hilda

As Christmas approached Hilda and I felt rather sad for not being at home. We decided to go to the Christmas carol service at King's College Chapel. Though we had to queue for hours, the music was so beautiful that we felt better just for being there.

By this time the rock and roll era had started and everyone was jiving to the music of Bill Haley and his band, jigging about in a cellar in Cambridge, getting squashed and shoved about. Very exciting it all was. One night at such a jazz session I met a boy who was sitting at a table, looking rather forlorn and wearing a rather strange, hand-knitted jumper. Hilda thought I should ask him to dance, which I did. This was quite forward really as in those days all nice girls waited to be asked. It turned out that he was studying German at a Cambridge college. We danced together several times and became friends.

Karin and Keith

As the May Ball season approached this student asked if I would like to go to a ball. I was so excited and couldn't believe my luck. With Hilda's help, I bought a white dress and thought I looked wonderful. We danced and ate and drank and punted on the river all night. It was marvellous. On another evening this student and I overstayed the 11 p.m. curfew time at his college and had to climb over the enormous college gates. I have looked at those gates since and wondered if I could have been that agile once. My children couldn't believe that I had done it, but I have proof, for my husband, who was that student, saw it all happening.

And so I completed my move from East to West, for I never returned to live in East Germany. And in the end the house in Goldschmiedenstrasse passed out of the family. Once my father and grandmother had died, my mother was living in the house alone, for my sister had moved to Wiesbaden and I was living in England. The house was in serious need of repairs, building materials were in short supply and my mother, being considered an enemy of the state and a bourgeois capitalist, was not a high priority customer. So she asked her cleaner, Frau T, if she would like the house. Frau T said she would ask her son. As a signed-up member of the Communist Party he could get materials for repairs and was very pleased to accept the offer. When Germany was reunited we were unable to put in a claim for compensation, as one could for any house occupied by strangers. Herr T later sold the house, which is now occupied by seven families. My grandmother would turn in her grave!

Revisiting Eisenach

The house in Goldschmiedenstrasse as it is now.

Wartburg Castle in Eisenach – famous as the place where Luther translated the Bible into German. Karin on right.

Eisenach school reunion of the class of 1950. Karin fourth from right.

Four girls from the class of 1950. From left, Mitte, Inge, Miechen and Karin.

ACKNOWLEDGEMENTS

With very many thanks to Audrey Talks for putting all these memories on to her computer, to Martin Talks who has the skill to turn these memories and photographs into this book and to Alphie Talks for designing the map.

Audrey and Karin

Produced by My Saga

www.my-saga.com

Tell your saga.

Printed in Great Britain
by Amazon